PEOPLE YOU SHOULD KNOW

ALEXANDRIA OCASIO-CORTEZ

Get to Know the Rising Politician

by Leticia Gonzales

Consultant:
Katherine Knutson
Professor of Political Science
Gustavus Adolphus College

CAPSTONE PRESS
a capstone imprint

Fact Finders Books are published by Capstone Press, an imprint of Capstone.
1710 Roe Crest Drive, North Mankato, Minnesota 56003
www.capstonepub.com

Library of Congress Cataloging-in-Publication Data is available on the Library of Congress website.
ISBN 978-1-5435-9089-0 (library binding)
ISBN 978-1-4966-6578-2 (paperback)
ISBN 978-1-5435-9090-6 (eBook PDF)

Summary: Alexandria Ocasio-Cortez, often known as AOC, wrote her name in the history books in 2018 when she became the youngest woman ever elected to the U.S. Congress. Her fearless, meteoric rise from paycheck-to-paycheck to the House of Representatives and her tireless advocacy for a world inclusive of all peoples will fascinate readers.

Image Credits
AP Photo: File/Jae C. Hong, 6; Getty Images: Corbis/Andrew Lichtenstein, 18; Library of Congress: 25; Newscom: AdMedia/CNP/Ron Sachs, 26, imageBROKER/Heiner Heine, 10, MEGA/NewYorkNewswire/Steve Sands, 5, Reuters/Joshua Roberts, 24, Sipa USA/Kristoffer Tripplaar, 22, Zuma Press/G. Ronald Lopez, 21; Shutterstock: Cory Seamer, 9, Crush Rush, 17, Joseph Sohm, 14, 15, Kletr, 11, Lev Radin, cover, Monkey Business Images, 16, Rachael Warriner, 29, Steve Edreff, 8; Wikimedia: Fletcher6, 13, U.S. House of Representatives, 4

Design Elements by Shutterstock

Editorial Credits
Jill Kalz, editor; Kayla Rossow, designer; Svetlana Zhurkin, media researcher; Tori Abraham, production specialist

Source Notes
page 6, line 10: Alexandra Ma and Eliza Relman. "Meet Alexandria Ocasio-Cortez, the Millennial, Socialist Political Novice Who's Now the Youngest Woman Ever Elected to Congress." Business Insider. https://www.businessinsider.com/all-about-alexandria-ocasio-cortez-who-beat-crowley-in-ny-dem-primary-2018-6. Accessed August 23, 2019.
page 11, line 15: David Remnick. "Alexandria Ocasio-Cortez's Historic Win and the Future of the Democratic Party." The New Yorker. https://www.newyorker.com/magazine/2018/07/23/alexandria-ocasio-cortezs-historic-win-and-the-future-of-the-democratic-party. Accessed August 23, 2019.
page 12, line 3: Kerri Anne Renzulli. "Alexandria Ocasio-Cortez Says Asking Herself This Question at 18 Changed the Direction of Her Life." CNBC. https://www.cnbc.com/2019/01/22/alexandria-ocasio-cortez-asking-myself-this-question-changed-my-life.html. Accessed August 23, 2019.
page 13, line 1: Kaitlyn Schallorn. "Who Is Alexandria Ocasio-Cortez? 5 Things to Know About the New York Congresswoman." Fox News. https://www.foxnews.com/politics/who-is-alexandria-ocasio-cortez-5-things-to-know-about-the-new-york-congresswoman. Accessed August 23, 2019.
page 14, line 9: Luka Mikeliones. "Ocasio-Cortez Calls to Abolish ICE, Says Latinos Must Be Exempt from Immigration Laws Because They Are 'Native' to U.S." Fox News. https://www.foxnews.com/politics/ocasio-cortez-calls-to-abolish-ice-says-latinos-must-be-exempt-from-immigration-laws-because-they-are-native-to-us. Accessed August 23, 2019.
page 16, line 6: Alex Morris. "Alexandria Ocasio-Cortez Wants the Country to Think Big." Rolling Stone. https://www.rollingstone.com/politics/politics-features/alexandria-ocasio-cortez-congress-interview-797214/. Accessed August 23, 2019.
page 18, line 3: Charlotte Alter. "'Change Is Closer Than We Think.' Inside Alexandria Ocasio-Cortez's Unlikely Rise." Time. http://time.com/longform/alexandria-ocasio-cortez-profile/. Accessed August 23, 2019.
page 24, line 13: Cady Lang. "Here's Why the Women of Congress Wore White for the 2019 State of the Union Address." Time. https://time.com/5518859/state-of-the-union-2019-white/. Accessed August 23, 2019.
page 29, line 1: Sarah Berger. "Alexandria Ocasio-Cortez: When You Only See 'White Dudes' Running the World, You Think You Need to Act Like One." CNBC. https://www.cnbc.com/2019/03/05/why-alexandria-ocasio-cortez-is-her-authentic-self-in-congress.html. Accessed August 23, 2019.

All internet sites appearing in back matter were available and accurate when this book was sent to press.

Printed in the United States of America.
PA99

TABLE OF CONTENTS

MAKING HISTORY

You may know her by three letters: AOC. It's a small abbreviation for a large, bright personality.

Alexandria Ocasio-Cortez (AOC) made U.S. history on November 6, 2018. That night she became the youngest woman ever elected to **Congress**. She was just 29 years old. She ran against Anthony Pappas in the **general election**. Not only did Alexandria beat him, she also won with an amazing 78 percent of the votes.

AOC's official U.S. Congress portrait, 2019

DID YOU KNOW?

The U.S. government is made up of three parts: legislative, executive, and judicial. The legislative branch makes the laws. It consists of the Senate and the House of **Representatives**, known together as Congress.

It wasn't the first time Alexandria had made history, though. Earlier, during the June **primary**, she beat Joseph Crowley. He served in the House of Representatives for 19 years. No one had run against him in a primary for 14 years. He was a powerful leader in Congress. Alexandria was an outsider.

AOC (front center) and others wore white the night of her general election win to honor women's right to vote.

Congress—the government body of the United States that makes laws, made up of the Senate and the House of Representatives

general election—a time during which voters choose which candidate representing different political parties will be elected

primary—an election in which voters choose which candidate will represent their political party in the general election

representative—a person elected to serve the government; U.S. representatives serve in the House of Representatives

Alexandria wasn't expected to win the general election. But she had a great strategy. Many younger people and first-time voters voted for her. She used technology and social media to deliver her messages. She connected with voters from different walks of life. She paid attention to people who spoke English as their second language. She listened to voters who worked more than one job.

People responded to her.

"Women like me aren't supposed to run for office," she said. "I wasn't born to a wealthy or powerful family."

After the 2018 primary win, AOC ramped up efforts to raise funds through personal appearances and social media.

Leading up to the election, many voters wanted a change. Only one in five members of Congress was a woman. About one in four members was under the age of 50. Because of these numbers, many women and young people decided to run for office in 2018. Getting elected would help them bring about the change they wanted.

The **campaigns** weren't easy. Alexandria and other women running for Congress faced extra challenges. People often notice what kind of clothing or makeup women are wearing before they listen to what the women are saying.

Women Representing

Along with Alexandria, a record number of women were elected to Congress. There were 127 combined in the U.S. Senate and House of Representatives. Ilhan Omar (Minnesota) and Rashida Tlaib (Michigan) were the first Muslim women elected. Deb Haaland (New Mexico) and Sharice Davids (Kansas) were the first Native American women elected.

campaign—organized actions and events with a specific goal, such as being elected

AN EDUCATION

Alexandria Ocasio-Cortez was born to Sergio Ocasio and Blanca Ocasio-Cortez on October 13, 1989, in the Bronx, New York City. Her mother grew up in Puerto Rico. Her father came from the South Bronx.

The couple worked hard to provide for Alexandria and her younger brother, Gabriel. Blanca worked two jobs, as a secretary and as a cleaning woman. Sergio worked as an architect.

AOC celebrated her heritage at the 2019 National Puerto Rican Day Parade in New York City.

DID YOU KNOW?

Puerto Rico is an island in the northeastern Caribbean Sea. It is an unincorporated territory of the United States, which means it governs itself but is part of the United States. Puerto Ricans are U.S. citizens.

The Bronx is the northernmost borough, or division, of New York City's five boroughs.

At first, home was the Parkchester community apartments in the Bronx. When Alexandria turned 5 years old, her parents moved the family to a **suburb** of New York City so Alexandria and her brother could attend a better school.

Some of Alexandria's teachers didn't believe she was very smart. She proved them wrong. In 2007, during her senior year of high school, she won second place in microbiology at the Intel International Science and Engineering Fair. Her project looked at the effect of substances called antioxidants on roundworms.

suburb—a community that lies right outside the city limits

Good grades earned Alexandria many **scholarships**. After graduating in 2007, she went to Boston University. Her dream was to be a doctor, specifically an obstetrician-gynecologist. She wanted to study women's health, including childbirth.

A study-abroad program to Africa gave AOC training at a local birthing clinic like this one.

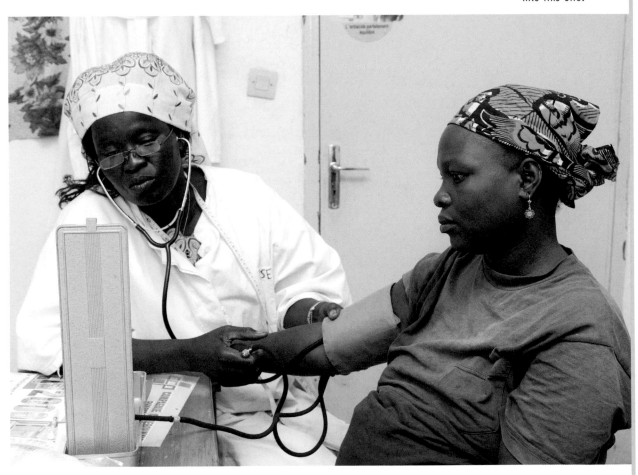

Alexandria took classes in biochemistry and spent time in West Africa to help deliver babies. But then she got sick with **malaria**. It causes high fever, chills, and sometimes death. Each year, hundreds of millions of people, worldwide, get malaria. Alexandria started thinking about how governments could help prevent it and diseases like it.

A female mosquito spreads malaria by feeding on infected blood and then biting another person.

Alexandria got better, but during her second year of college, she got terrible news. Her father had lung cancer. He died at the age of 48.

"My mother was done. My brother was lost," said Alexandria. "I took it hard, too, but I channeled it into my studies. That's how I dealt with it. I was home for a week and went right back to school. The last thing my father had told me in the hospital was 'Make me proud.'"

malaria—a sometimes-deadly disease spread by mosquitoes
scholarship—an award to help pay for schooling

3 ⟩ CHOOSING A PATH

After her father's death, Alexandria looked at her own life differently.

"It really clarified a lot of things, because having my father pass away at such a young age forced a lot of questions of mortality. What am I here for?" she asked.

She wasn't sure if she still wanted to go to medical school and become a doctor. She wanted to help a greater number of people at once, rather than one at a time. Politics had always been a part of Alexandria's family. So, she changed her studies to **economics** and **international relations**.

DID YOU KNOW?

In 2011, Alexandria received a Bachelor of Arts (B.A.) degree with two majors from Boston University—Economics and International Relations. She graduated "cum laude," meaning her grades were in the top 15 to 30 percent of her class.

"Politics were talked about at the table every single day," she said. "It's the culture. In Puerto Rico, you talk about politics all the time, even when people disagree."

Most of AOC's college classes were held in the College of Arts and Sciences buildings on the Boston University campus.

economics—the study of how money is produced and shared
international relations—the study of politics and geography around the world

Alexandria started putting her political studies to use right away. She worked part-time for Senator Edward (Ted) Kennedy. He was a **Democrat** from Massachusetts. Alexandria worked on **immigration** cases. Helping people who were new to the country inspired her to do more hands-on work in the community.

"We have to have respect for children, respect for families, respect for human rights, and respect for the right of human mobility," she said.

In 2008, AOC went on to help another Democrat, presidential hopeful Barack Obama.

In 2008, Alexandria served as a volunteer for Democrat Barack Obama's presidential campaign. She made countless phone calls, urging people to vote. She shared Obama's campaign message of "Yes, We Can!" The slogan meant that if people worked together, they could make the great changes they wanted to see.

The "Yes, We Can!" slogan brought together voters of all races and backgrounds.

Democrat—a member of the Democratic political party, one of the two major parties in the United States

immigration—the act of moving from one country to live permanently in another

15

FINDING HER VOICE

Alexandria graduated from Boston University in 2011. For a few years, she worked odd jobs to help support her mother. She worked as a bartender at a restaurant in New York City. She learned a lot about people and politics there.

The largest group of minimum-wage earners in the United States works in the restaurant industry. They number nearly 11 million.

"The thing that people don't understand about restaurants is that they're one of the most political environments," said Alexandria. "You're shoulder-to-shoulder with immigrants. . . . Your hourly wage is even less than the minimum wage. You're working for tips."

Bernie Sanders ran for U.S. president in 2016. He eventually lost the Democratic nomination to Hillary Clinton.

Building on her strong political interests, Alexandria worked as an organizer for Senator Bernie Sanders' 2016 presidential campaign. Bernie had served as a U.S. senator for the state of Vermont since 2007. Alexandria believed in many of the things Bernie stood for, including better health care for all Americans.

Working on Bernie's campaign lit a new fire inside Alexandria.

"I had done grassroots organizing before," Alexandria said. "But Sanders' race was one of my first times where I crossed that bridge from grassroots community organizing to [higher-level] organizing."

Alexandria raised money for supplies for **activists**. She spoke out at the Standing Rock Indian Reservation in North Dakota in 2016. **Protesters** there were upset about the Dakota Access Pipeline. They worried that oil from the pipes would leak out and ruin the area's drinking water.

"Water protectors" celebrated a short-lived stop in construction of the Dakota Access Pipeline in late 2016. Work eventually continued, with the pipeline being completed in 2017.

On Alexandria's drive back to New York from North Dakota, a group called Brand New Congress contacted her. They asked her to run for office. The group was created by former members of Bernie Sanders' staff. They had learned about Alexandria from a letter from her brother. Gabriel told the group that his sister would make the perfect candidate.

DID YOU KNOW?

An organizer brings people together for events or to bring in voters. To organize at a "grassroots" level means to work at a basic level with ordinary, everyday citizens, rather than a large, well-funded political party.

activist—a person who works for social or political change
protester—someone who speaks out about something strongly and publicly

Alexandria decided to run for Congress in early 2017. She was a member of the Democratic Socialists of America (DSA). The DSA is a group that believes the people, not large businesses, should decide how to run society. Workers themselves should own the businesses in which they work.

Alexandria's campaign for Congress focused on people from the working class. She believed that all citizens should have medical, dental, vision, and mental health insurance. She also supported free college for everyone. She felt everyone should have proper housing. Creating jobs that paid at least $15 an hour was also important to her. Alexandria wanted to get rid of the Immigration and Customs Enforcement Office (ICE), which enforces immigration laws in the United States.

Alexandria's opponent in the primary, Joseph Crowley, didn't seem to take her run for office seriously. He participated in just one political debate with her. According to his spokesperson, Joseph missed two other debates because of scheduling conflicts.

During her 2018 primary campaign, AOC painted Joseph Crowley as someone who served big business rather than his voters.

He Said, She Said

Political debates are an important part of an election. They give candidates a chance to talk about the issues that are important to voters. Voters can also see what kind of leader each candidate would be if he or she were elected.

Alexandria's campaign workers were mostly new to campaigning. As a result, they raised much less money than Joseph Crowley's team did. Alexandria didn't accept money from corporate political action committees (PACs), either. It was a way to show she couldn't be swayed to vote a certain way simply because of money.

Although her campaign wasn't well-funded, Alexandria proved strong. Her campaign posters were inspired by well-known activists such as Cesar Chavez and Dolores Huerta. They used bold lettering and colorful artwork. Posters were also printed in both English and Spanish.

Alexandria used vivid photography and web videos to educate voters. Her team made phone calls and went door-to-door to share her message. With the help of these tools, Alexandria won 56.7 percent of the vote, beating Joseph Crowley by 4,018 votes.

President Barack Obama awarded Dolores Huerta the Presidential Medal of Freedom in 2012 for her activist work.

After her victory in the primary, people were excited to get Alexandria elected. They donated money and volunteered their time. Alexandria also traveled around the United States to encourage people to vote for other young candidates like her. In the general election in November, Alexandria won against **Republican** Anthony Pappas and became the youngest woman ever elected to Congress.

Workers' Rights

Cesar Chavez (1927–1993) was a Latino-American civil rights leader who fought, in nonviolent ways, for better working conditions and fair wages for farm workers. He joined forces with fellow Latino-American activist Dolores Huerta (1930–) in 1962 to form the National Farm Workers Association (later named the United Farm Workers [UFW] union). UFW continues to protect the rights of farm workers to this day.

Republican—a member of the Republican political party, one of the two major parties in the United States

Alexandria wasn't the only one to make history on the night of November 6, 2018. The 116th Congress was made up of people from many races and backgrounds. The group of lawmakers included 116 people who were black, Hispanic, Asian/Pacific Islander, and Native American.

Alexandria used her win to make a statement for other women whenever possible. When she was officially sworn in on January 3, 2019, she wore a white suit. "I wore all-white today to honor the women who paved the path before me, and for all the women yet to come," she said. "From **suffragettes** to Shirley Chisholm, I wouldn't be here if it wasn't for the mothers of the movement."

AOC was sworn in alongside her mother and Speaker of the House Nancy Pelosi (far left).

Alexandria often wore hoop earrings and red lipstick to show support for Sonia Sotomayor, the first Hispanic person and third woman to serve on the U.S. Supreme Court. When Sonia was named to the court in 2009, she had been told not to stand out. She was allowed to wear only neutral-colored nail polish.

Famous Firsts

Shirley Chisholm became the first black woman elected to Congress in 1968. She was also the first woman and the first black woman to seek the nomination for U.S. president from one of the two major political parties. She did so in 1972 but did not succeed.

Shirley Chisholm

In 1989, Ileana Ros-Lehtinen became the first Latina woman elected to Congress. She was also the first Cuban American to serve.

The youngest black woman elected to Congress was Lauren Underwood. She was elected at the same time as Alexandria. She was 32 years old.

suffragette—a woman who fought for women's right to vote

After being sworn in, Alexandria got to work fast. She served on several committees, including the House Oversight and Reform committee. It oversees **fraud** and abuse-of-power investigations within the government. She also served on the House Financial Services committee. It oversees the financial services industry, including banks and insurance companies.

Although new and the youngest member of Congress, AOC spoke up in meetings and didn't shy away from asking tough questions.

Alexandria promised to pay her support team a good wage. Many government staffers work long hours. They have high expenses, living in Washington, D.C. Some staffers make as little as $35,000 a year.

Alexandria knew what it was like to struggle. She'd grown up watching her mother work two jobs to pay the bills. Alexandria herself didn't have health insurance and couldn't afford a place to live until after she started working in the U.S. government. She didn't get paid in the three months between being elected and being sworn in. She had quit her part-time bartending job in early 2018 to campaign. She was also still paying off her college loans. In many ways, Alexandria's life represented the lives of the people who had voted for her.

fraud—the practice of cheating or tricking people

Alexandria wanted real change, especially for working-class people. Her first proposal, H.Res. 109, called for the federal government to create a Green New Deal. The program would focus on the following goals:

- getting rid of greenhouse gases, to fight climate change;
- providing high-wage jobs and economic well-being for everyone;
- improving the nation's roads, bridges, and buildings;
- ensuring a healthy environment for all, including clean air and water, healthy food, and access to nature;
- making sure everyone is treated fairly and equally.

Alexandria continued to use social media to connect with voters after she was elected. Live feeds on Instagram showed videos of her potting plants and cooking meals. Some people, including fellow politicians, made fun of the videos. Others saw the videos as proof that Alexandria was just a regular person, doing regular things.

AOC presented her ideas for a Green New Deal at a town hall meeting in 2019.

"One way that we can really change leadership is by being ourselves as we are," Alexandria said. "Because whether you're 15 or whether you're 50 or whether you're 100 years old, there's always people looking at you to try and figure out how to navigate their life."

Many have tried, and will likely continue to try, to hold Alexandria back. But this rising politician shows no signs of slowing anytime soon.

GLOSSARY

activist (AK-tih-vehst)—a person who works for social or political change

campaign (kam-PAYN)—organized actions and events with a specific goal, such as being elected

Congress (KAHN-grehs)—the government body of the United States that makes laws, made up of the Senate and the House of Representatives

Democrat (DEH-muh-krat)—a member of the Democratic political party, one of the two major parties in the United States; Democrats are viewed as more progressive, supporting social and economic equality; they also believe the government should use more control with the economy, but less in private affairs

economics (ek-uh-NAH-miks)—the study of how money is produced and shared

fraud (FRAWD)—the practice of cheating or tricking people

general election (JEN-ruhl uh-LEK-shun)—a time during which voters choose which candidate representing different political parties will be elected

immigration (im-uh-GRAY-shun)—the act of moving from one country to live permanently in another

international relations (in-tur-NASH-uh-nuhl reh-LAY-shunz)—the study of politics and geography around the world

malaria (muh-LAIR-ee-uh)—a sometimes-deadly disease spread by mosquitoes

primary (PRY-mair-ee)—an election in which voters choose which candidate will represent their political party in the general election

protester (PRO-tess-tuhr)—someone who speaks out about something strongly and publicly

representative (rep-ri-ZEN-tuh-tiv)—a person elected to serve the government; U.S. representatives serve in the House of Representatives

Republican (reh-PUHB-leh-kehn)—a member of the Republican political party, one of the two major parties in the United States; Republicans believe in conservative social policies, low taxes, and that the government should stay out of the economy

scholarship (SKAHL-uhr-ship)—an award to help pay for schooling

suburb (SUH-burb)—a community that lies right outside the city limits

suffragette (SUHF-ruh-jet)—a woman who fought for women's right to vote

READ MORE

Calvert, Jennifer. *Teen Trailblazers: 30 Fearless Girls Who Changed the World Before They Were 20.* New York: Castle Point, 2018.

Hopkinson, Deborah. *What Is the Women's Rights Movement?* New York: Penguin Workshop, 2018.

Rajczak Nelson, Kristen. *Who Can Vote?* New York: PowerKids Press, 2019.

INTERNET SITES

Ben's Guide to the U.S. Government
https://bensguide.gpo.gov

Ducksters Site: U.S. Government for Kids
https://www.ducksters.com/history/us_government.php

KidCitizen
https://www.kidcitizen.net

Kids in the House
https://kids-clerk.house.gov

CRITICAL THINKING QUESTIONS

1. Think about Alexandria's childhood. How did her upbringing and education shape her into the adult she is now?

2. Not many people expected Alexandria to win her first election. Think about a time when you met a challenge, something other people didn't think you could do. What did you learn about yourself during the experience?

3. Alexandria made history with her unexpected win in 2018. Years from now, what would you want people to remember and admire you for?

INDEX